Python Data Sc

Programming Languages Project

Table of Contents

Introduction

Congratulations on purchasing *Python Data Science* and thank you for doing so.

The following chapters will discuss everything that we need to know when it comes to data science and how to complete the process of data science with Python. There are so many different parts that come together when we work on data science, but if you are able to put it all together, and work to really analyze the informations that you have to beat out the competition, you will find that data science with Python can be the right move for you.

The beginning of this guidebook is going to spend some time looking at data science. We will explore how so many businesses will take the time to gather up informations, usually from a variety of sources, and then will be unsure of what they should do with that information once they have collected it. We can then take a look at the data life cycle and how we can take that information, clean it off, analyze it, and come up with insights and predictions that help grow our business more than ever before.

With that in mind, it is time to move on to some of the basics of Python that we need to know. We can certainly choose from many different options when it comes to data science, but none are going to be as effective and as easy to work with as the Python language. We will spend this time looking what Python is about, how to download the program on your chosen operating system, and some of the basics that come with coding in Python.

From there, we will take a closer look at some of the different libraries that we are able to bring into the mix to see the best results with data science and the Python library. There is a lot that we are able to do with the traditional Python library to see results, but when we are able to add in some of the Python libraries that have been designed to work with data science, the power and strength that comes with our algorithms and models will help with this as well.

With the right coding language ready and some good data science libraries, there are a few more topics that we need to discuss when it comes to working with data science. We will look at some of the common tasks that we are able to do with data science, the different data types that work with here, and the future of data science and where this industry is going to head in the future, and what we should expect.

There is so much that can come into play when we work with data science, and it is one of the best ways for a business to differentiate from the competition and actually see some results in the process. And the Python language is a great option to learn to help us analyze and create a model that works with the info that we have. When we are ready to learn more about data science, and how to use the Python coding language to go with it, make sure to check out this guidebook to help you get started.

With so many books around with the same subject, we are happy you are reading ours! We gathered the most useful and entertaining information found for the topic. Without further ado, please enjoy!

Chapter 1: What is Data Science?

One of the biggest buzzwords in the business right now is the idea of data science. This is a process that so many businesses want to get ahold of. They know the importance of collecting informations, but as they are able to collect so much in a short period of time, they are also curious as to what is the next step. Data science is going to include all of the different steps that you take with the data. It includes collecting and cleaning it if it comes from more than one source, analyzing and usually with machine learning algorithms and models, and then presenting your findings from the analysis with some good data visualizations.

Data science is considered the detailed study that a business can go through, no matter what industry they are in, to look at how the flow of information from all of the data they have collected and stored can be used to help the business succeed, come up with some new products, beat out the competition, and really make their customers happy. It is going to involve a lot of different steps, but usually starts out with the company obtaining any kind of insights and trends out of data, usually raw and unstructured info, and then they can use these insights to make smarter business decisions.

The neat thing to remember here is that there really is a ton that we are able to do with the process of data science, and as a whole, it is going to make life a lot easier for your whole business. Since most businesses that would use data science are already in the process of collecting large amounts of data on their customers on a regular basis, this first step may already be done.

However, we have to remember that just going out and collecting the data is not enough, no matter how much info we end up collecting. You have to actually be able to take all of that data and perform an analysis on it, and learn from that information, otherwise, the data is useless to your business and your business goals overall.

As many companies have already seen, we live in a modern world where so much of what we do is moving over to the digital world. This means that most of these companies are going to be overloaded with a ton of data. Sometimes these informations comes to us with a structure, but there is a lot of unstructured data that we may need to sort through as well because it saves money and it is easier to manage and use.

In addition, some of the technologies that are being developed and used more often are enabling us to find smarter and even cost-saving methods to hold onto and store data, which is going to make it so much easier than ever for any company who wants, to gather a large amount of this informations and use it to improve themselves.

When it comes to the locations and sources where a business can collect this data there are actually quite a few options that are open to the business. Many businesses will hire data scientists to help them collect this information from sources like social media, sensors, digital videos and pictures, purchased transactions that they get from their customers and even from surveys that the customers may have taken.

Because there are so many sources that the company is able to focus on when it comes to getting the information they want, it won't take much research before the company becomes flooded with all of the presented data. There is just so much data available, which is great, but we have to make sure that we know the right steps to handle the info and to learn what is there, rather than just collecting the information and calling it good.

The analysis that you will do on all of that data that comes in is a big part of data science. All this helps us to bring together a lot of professional skills in order to handle that info and put it to good use. Yes, it is going to include searching for the info so it is a good idea to not forget it or skip over this part, but it can come in and help with understanding the info as well. To get all of this done, we need to have a few skills come together, either in one person or within the team, to make data science useful. Some of the things that data science, and the info we collect, will be able to help us out with will include.

1. Reducing the number of costs that the business has to deal with.
2. Helping to launch a brand new service or product and knowing it will do well.

3. To help gauge the effectiveness that we see in a new marketing campaign.
4. To help tap into some different demographics along the way.
5. To ensure that we can get into a new market and see success.

Of course, this is not an extensive list that we can look at, and knowing the right steps and all of the benefits that come with working in data science can really help us to see some improvements and can make the business grow. No matter what items or services you sell, what your geographic location is, or what industry you are in you can use data science in order to help your business become more successful.

Sometimes, it is hard for companies to really see how they can use data science to help improve themselves. We may assume that this is just a bunch of hype, or that only a few companies have really been able to see success with it. However, there are a ton of companies that are able to use this kind of information to get themselves ahead, including some of the big names like Amazon, Visa, and Google. While your business may or may not be on the same level as those three, it is still possible for you to put data science to work for your needs, improving what you can offer on the market, how you can help customers out, and so much more.

It is important to note that data science is a field that is already taking over the world, and it is helping companies in many different areas. For example, it is showing companies the best way to grow, how to reach their customers in the correct and most efficient manner, how to find new sources of value, and so much more. It often depends on the overall goal of the company for using this process of data science to determine what they will get out of it.

With all of the benefits that come with using this process of data science, and all of the big-name companies who are jumping on board and trying to gain some of the knowledge and benefits as well, it is important for us to take a look at the life cycle that comes with data science, and the steps that it takes to make this project a big success. Let's dive into some of the things that we need to know about the data life cycle so we know the basics of what needs to happen to see success with data science.

Data discovery

The first step that we are going to see with this life cycle is the idea that companies need to get out there and actually discover the info they want to use. This is the phase where we will search in a lot of different sources in order to discover the data that we need. Sometimes the data is going to be structured, such as in text format but other times it may come in a more unstructured format like videos and images. There are even some times when the data we find comes to us as a relational database system instead.

These are going to be considered some of the more traditional ways that you can collect the info that you need, but it is also possible for an organization to explore some different options as well. For example, many companies are relying on social media to help them reach their customers and to gain a better understanding of the mindset and buying decisions of these customers through this option.

Often this phase is going to include us starting out with a big question that we would like answered, and then searching either for the data in the first place or if we already have the data, searching through the info that we have already collected. This makes it easier for us to get through all of that data and actually gain the insights that we are looking for.

Getting the data prepared

After we spend some time going through all of the different sources to find the information that we need, it is time to actually look at how we can use this data, and data preparation will help out with this. There are a few steps that happen in this phase, basically we are going to do things like converting the informations from all of those different sources into one common format so that they work together, and an algorithm that we pick out later will be able to handle the data without errors or mistakes.

This process is going to be more involved, but it is where the data scientist will start collecting clean subsets of data and then will insert the defaults and the parameters that are needed for you. In some cases, the methods that you use will be more complex, like identifying some of the values that are missing out of that data, and more.

Another step that needs to happen while you are here is to clean off the data. This is so important when you collect the data from more than one source because it ensures that it's the same and that the algorithm you pick will be able to read it all later. You also want to make sure that there isn't any informations missing, that the duplicate values are gone, and there is nothing else found within the set of data you want to work with that will decrease the accuracy of the model that you are trying to make.

After you go through and clean off the data you would like to use, the next step is to do the integration and then create our own conclusion based on the set of data for the analysis. This analysis is going to involve taking the data and then merging two or more tables together that have the same objects, but different information. It can also include the process of aggregation, which is when we summarize the different fields found in the table as we go through the process.

During this whole process, the goal is for us to explore and then come up with an understanding of the patterns, as well as the values, that are going to show up in the data set that we are working with. This can take some time and some patience, but it is going to ensure that any mathematical models we work with later make sense and work the way that we want.

Mathematical models

When working with data science, all of the projects that you will want to work with will need to use mathematical models to help them get it all done. These are models that we can plan out ahead of time and then the data scientist is going to build them up to help suit the needs of the business or the question that they would like answered. In some cases, it is possible to work with a few different areas that fall in the world of mathematics, including linear regression, statistics, and logistics, to get these models done.

To get all of this done, we also have to make sure we are using the right tools and methods to make it easier. Some of the computing tools for statistics that come with R can help as well as working with some other advanced analytical tools, SQL, and Python, and any visualization tool that you need to make sure the data makes sense.

Also, we have to make sure that we are getting results that are satisfactory out of all the work and sometimes that means we need to bring in more than one algorithm or model to see the results. In this case, the data scientist has to go through and create a group of models that can work together to go through that info and answer any of the questions that the business has.

After measuring out the models that they would like to use, the data scientist can then revise some of the parameters that are in place, and do the fine-tuning that is needed as they go through the next round of modeling. This process is going to take up a few rounds to complete because you have to test it out more than once to make sure that it's going to work the way that you would like it to.

Putting it all into action

At this point, we have had a chance to prepare the data the way that it needs to be done, and we have been able to build up some of the models that we want to us. With this in mind, it is time to work with the models to get them to provide us with the kinds of results that need to show up. It is possible, depending on the data you have the model you choose to go with, that there will be a few discrepancies, and you may have to go through a few levels of troubleshooting to deal with the process, but this is normal. Most data scientists have to make some changes to their models as they go through the process before coming up with the solution that is right for them.

Of course, to really see how the model is going to play out in the real world, we need to first test out the model. This is the best way to see what will happen when the model is in use, rather than just a theory. You can try out a new algorithm with it as well to see if one type is a better option than any of the others. Sometimes, this is the part where we will decide to put in more than one algorithm to handle our data needs.

The importance of communication

While we are going through this life cycle of data, we need to spend a few moments talking about how important communication can be to the whole process. A good data scientist, or a good team of data scientists, are not going to be just working with the algorithms and the numbers; they are also going to handle the communication that has to go on. There is someone on the business end, such as the marketers and key decision-makers who will need to be able to read through this information, and the data scientist needs to be able to communicate in a manner that is easy to understand.

Communicating what has been found inside of the data, and through the various algorithms used, is going to be one of the important steps that we need to use in the data life cycle. During this stage, the professional is going to be able to talk between the different teams that are present, and they have to be skilled enough to communicate and to share their findings in a clear and concise manner.

There are many different people who need to have this kind of information, and not all of them are going to be data scientists or people who can understand some of the technical parts that come into play. The data scientist still has to share this information to make sure that these key decision-makers are able to understand the information and what insights have been found in the data. The decision-makers can then take that information and use it to decide which direction to take their company.

One thing to keep in mind here though is that a data scientist has to make sure that they are doing this communication in many different ways. Often this can include the written and the spoken word, so get ready to work on some of those public speaking skills and interpersonal skills to get things done.

But the written and the spoken words are not going to be the only places where the data scientist is going to need to know how to communicate. For example, the last part that comes with data science and its lifecycle is some kind of visualization of the information and the insights that are found in all that data. These visualizations can take all of the numbers and all of the data, and put it into some kind of image, like a bar chart, a graph, a pie chart or some other method or image.

This is useful because it can take a large amount of informations and put it into a form that we are able to just glance at and understand. Instead of having to go through all of the different pieces of information, and reading through all of that data, we can use these images to make it easier to see and understand what is going on, what relationships showed up for each part, and so much more.

The data life cycle is so important to help you understand what is in all of that data that you have collected over time. Companies are able to collect more data than ever, but they need to know how to take it and turn it into a form that can actually be used. This is often easier said than done, but by working with the life cycle of data that we talked about previously, you will be able to not only collect all of the data but also put it to good use to make some good business decisions.

Chapter 2: The Python Coding Language

Now that we know a bit more about the idea that comes with data science, it is time for us to explore a bit about Python and what is included with this kind of language. You will find that there is a variety of options when it comes to coding and programming, and it often depends on what you would like to accomplish with your work. Some people like to spend more time working on websites and creating content online and Java is a good option for that. Then there are options that are a bit more traditional, ones that work for specific projects, and even some that are made to handle databases and other similar work.

And then there is the Python language. This language is often considered one of the best coding languages that you can work with because of all the features that come with it, the kind of power that is provided, and the ease of use for beginners who are just learning how to code. There are a lot of benefits that will come with using this kind of coding language, so making sure that we understand how this works, and some of the benefits that come with Python can be important too.

There are a lot of different benefits that you are going to see when it comes to working with the Python language, and learning how to use it can be in your advantage overall. Some of the reasons that programmers like to work with this kind of coding language over some of the other options out there will include the following:

1. There are a lot of libraries that can connect with Python. There is already a lot that you can do with the regular library that comes with Python. But there are a few capabilities that are missing. The good news here is that many extensions and other libraries out there are set up to work with Python, and fill in where some of these capabilities are missing. We will talk about a few of the best libraries that you can use to help out with things like machine learning and data science later in this guidebook.

2. Integration features. Python is set up to work with many different coding languages as well. This can be useful with some of the different machine learning libraries that we are going to add on later

and can bring even more power to what we can do with some of our codes here.

3. More productivity for the programmer: The Python language has a lot of designs that are object-oriented and a lot of support libraries. Because of all these resources and how easy it is to use the program, the programmer is going to increase their productivity. This can even be used to help improve the productivity of the programmer while using languages like C#, C++, C, Perl, VB, and even Java.

4. Easy to learn: Python was developed to be easy to use and easily adaptable. This translates into being easy, even for a beginner to learn. This guidebook will focus on some of the basics that you can learn with Python, but by the time you are done, you will have the ability to write some powerful codes and even do some of your own projects!

5. The language is easy to read: As you go through this guidebook, you will quickly see that the codes are easy to read. There isn't a ton of extras in the code with things that you just don't understand. It won't take long until you are able to read through some of the codes on your own. Before you even go through and learn what everything means, take a look through some of the codes in this guidebook, you may be surprised to see that the

words are in English and even though you don't fully understand what they say right away you can at least understand the words.

6. You still get a lot of power with all of the codings that you do. Even with all of the simplicity of use that we have from the Python code, you will find that it is still going to have all of the power that you need to see results. As a beginner language, many of those who start out with the worry that it is too simple to handle some of the work they need to complete. But you will quickly find that Python, whether you add on the extensions and libraries or not, will still have a lot of the power that you are looking for.

7. A great community. Because of all the benefits that we just listed above, there are many people who are interested in working on the Python coding language for their coding needs. These people come from all around the world, with varying degrees of programming skills to work with as well. This is great news for people who are just getting started with this language because it allows them to find lots of resources for handling different projects, troubleshooting help and more.

With this in mind, we need to move on and look at some of the steps that you can take to install the Python language on your computer, and actually get it to work well. We are going to download Python from www.python.org. There are other options to go with, but this website gives us all of the files and folders that we need for Python to work, and we can download them all for free. If you would like a special library or some special third party options, then you can download from there, but remember to check that it comes with an IDLE and all the other parts, or the program will not work for you.

Python is able to work on all of the major operating systems including Linux, Windows, and Mac so we are going to take a few minutes to look at how you can download this system on all three of these, based on which operating system you choose to work with.

To start o with, we are going to look at how to download Python on a Mac OS X system. If you are working with the Mac operating system, you can go ahead and look and notice how Python 2 is already installed on the system. The exact version that we see with this is going to depend on how new or old your computer is, but there will be some version of this already on there. You can choose to stay with this and work with Python 2, but for most of the work that you need to do with data science and machine learning, the libraries will require you to have one of the Python 3 versions so it is best to just upgrade now. To check to see if there is a Python 3 installation on the computer, open up your terminal app, and then type in the following prompt:

Python3 – V

The default that you are going to find on this kind of system is that Python 3 is not going to be there at all, and you will have to go through the whole process of installing Python 3 to get it to work. The good thing here though is that you can simply go to the www.python.org website that we listed above, and everything will be downloadable from that website onto your Mac computer.

Being able to run the IDLE and the Python shell is going to depend on which version you choose and some of your own personal preferences. You can use the following commands to help you start the shell and IDLE applications:

- For Python 2.X just type in "Idle"
- For Python 3.X, just type in "idle3"

If you followed all of the installation steps that came from the website, you should end up with the Python 3 version of your choice on your computer, along with the shell, the IDLE, and any of the other parts that you need all in one. Now you are able to use Python on your Mac computer.

Now, it is possible that you will have a computer with a Windows operating system and you want to make sure that you can get the Python language on this computer. You will not find a version of this program on your Windows system unless you bought it from someone who installed it themselves. Windows has its own programming language that comes pre-installed, so you have to go through a few steps in order to get Python on your computer and ready to go.

Do not worry though. Even without Python being already on the computer, and even with Windows having its own version of a programming language present, Python is going to work just fine on this kind of operating system. We just need to make sure that we add in all of the right parts, including the necessary environment variables, to help all of the scripts for Python to work in the way that we want. Some of the steps that you need to take to make sure the Python language works on a Windows Operating System will include:

1. To set this up, you need to visit the official Python download page and grab the Windows installer. You can choose to do the latest version of Python 3, or go with another option. By default, the installer is going to provide you with the 32-bit version of Python, but you can choose to switch this to the 64-bit version if you wish. The 32-bit is often best to make sure that there are not any compatibility issues with the older packages, but you can experiment if you'd like to.
2. Now right-click on the installer and select "Run as Administrator". There are going to be two options to choose from. You will want to pick out "Customize Installation"
3. On the following screen, make sure all of the boxes under "Optional Features" are clicked and then click to move on.

4. While under Advanced Options" you should pick out the location where you want Python to be installed. Click on Install. Give it some time to finish and then close the installer.
5. Next, set the PATH variable for the system so that it includes directories that will include packages and other components that you will need later. To do this use the following instructions:
   a. Open up the Control Panel. Do this by clicking on the taskbar and typing in Control Panel. Click on the icon.
   b. Inside the Control Panel, search for Environment. Then click on Edit the System Environment Variables. From here, you can click on the button for Environment Variables.
   c. Go to the section for User Variables. You can either edit the PATH variable that is there, or you can create one.
   d. If there is not a variable for PATH on the system, then create one by clicking on New. Make the name for the PATH variable and add in the directories that you want. Click on close all the control Panel dialogs and move on.
6. Now you can open up your command prompt. Do this by clicking on Start Menu, then Windows System, and then Command Prompt. Type in "python". This is going to load up the Python interpreter for you.

When you get to this point, all of the steps should be done so that you can open up the program and write out the codes that you want to use with this language. You can open up the interpreter, the shell, and all of the other parts and get started with writing your codes in no time!

And finally, we need to take a moment to look and see how we can install the Python version that we want on a Linux system. This one may not have quite the popularity that we see with some of the other two, but it is still a great operating system to work with, especially when it comes to coding. Moreover, working and installing Python on this operating system is often easier than we may think.

The first thing that we want to do if we have a Linux operating system is check to see whether or not Python is already on the computer. To do this, we want to open up the command prompt on Linux, and then work with the code below to help us out:

$ python3 - - version

If you are on Ubuntu 16.10 or newer, then it is a simple process to install Python 3.6. you just need to use the following commands:

```
$ sudo apt-get update
$ sudo apt-get install Python3.6
```

If you are relying on an older version of Ubuntu or another version, then you may want to work with the deadsnakes PPA, or another tool, to help you download the Python 3.6 version. The code that you need to do this includes:

```
$ sudo apt-get install software-properties-common
$ sudo add-apt repository ppa:deadsnakes/ppa
# suoda apt-get update
$ sudo apt-get install python3.6
```

The good thing to remember here is that if you have worked with some of the other Linux distributions in the past, it is likely that you have a version of Python installed on the system, and you do not even need to go through some of these simple steps. If you do not have Python on your computer, you can use the package manager for the distribution. You can also choose to go through the steps above if you do not like the version of Python that is already in the Linux operating system when you start.

Chapter 3: Some of the Basic Coding in Python

Before we move on to some of the libraries that we can use when it comes to data science, we first need to take a look at some of the basics that are going to show up in our Python code. These basics are so important because they help us to really make sure that we understand what is going on in some of the codes that we write and they will ensure that we are able to get familiar with Python coding as a whole. Some of the basics that we need to take a look at when it comes to coding in Python will include:

The keywords in Python

The first place we need to start from, when it comes to coding in Python is to take look at the keywords. These keywords are important because they are going to be held back from being used in other parts of the code. The Python compiler needs these words to help it know what commands you would like to see executed. If you put these into other parts of the code, you are going to be an error message because the compiler is not certain what you would like to see it do for you. Some of the keywords that you need to be careful about when working in Python will include:

- Except
- Else
- If
- Yield
- Assert
- Elif
- From
- Try
- While
- Lambda
- For
- Continue
- None
- False
- Class
- Finally
- Is
- Return
- Pass
- Or
- Not
- With

How to name the identifiers

We need to take a quick look at some of the steps that you have to remember if you run across an identifier and you need to name it. There are a few different types of identifiers that we need to focus on, including variables, entities, functions, and classes, and we will talk about a few of these in a moment. But all of them are going to follow the same rules so this makes things a little bit easier as well.

There are a lot of different options that can come up when it is time to name your identifiers, which can make it a lot easier to work with overall. You will be able to choose any kind of letter that you would like, any number, and you can add in the underscore symbol to the name as well. You should also go with something that makes sense for that part of the code, and that you will be able to remember so you can pull it out later.

You do have a few restrictions that we need to keep in mind here too. You cannot start out the name of your identifier with a number, and you cannot add in spaces to the mix either. So, it is not found to write out something like 3 words or three words for the name, but you would be fine writing out something like three words or three_words to get the name of the identifier to work.

Working with the comments

Another part of the puzzle that we need to take a look at here in the comments. There may be times when you are writing out some part of the code, and you will want to add in a nice note or an explanation about what you are doing in this part of the code for someone who may be looking it over. Nevertheless, you want to be able to add in these notes without messing up the code or making a glitch happen. This is where the comments are able to help us out.

With the comments, you can add in any notes or explanations that you would like to the code without having to worry about messing it up at all. You just need to use the # symbol before your note and the compiler knows that it should just skip over this part.

You can add in as many or as few of these comments as you would like, but it is generally best if you can keep your use of these down to a minimum so that you do not make the code look as messy.

The variables

Variables are another part of the code that you will need to know about because they are so common in your code. The variables are there to help store some of the values that you place in the code, helping them to stay organized and nice. You can easily add in some of the values to the right variable simply by using the equal sign. It is even possible for you to take two values and add them to the same variables if you want and you will see this occur in a few of the codes that we discuss through this guidebook. Variables are very common and you will easily see them throughout the examples that we show.

Assigning a value over to a variable

One of the things that we need to know before we jump into some of the libraries is an idea of how to assign a value over to one of the variables that you are working with. This is a simple process, but we want to make sure that we are doing it in the proper manner, and that this will all work out when coding. There are many times, whether you are doing machine learning or something a bit easier, where you will need to make sure that a value is assigned to your variable, and doing it the right way will ensure that you save the right spot of memory on the computer and that you are easily able to pull that value back up later.

As you do some work with your variables, you will find that these values are going to show up in three options. Each of these options is going to be useful at some point and it really depends on the code type that you are trying to write in the process and the value that comes with it. The different types of variables that you can work with will include:

- Float: this would include numbers like 3.14 and so on.
- String: this is going to be like a statement where you could write out something like "Thank you for visiting my page!" or another similar phrase.

- Whole number: this would be any of the other numbers that you would use that do not have a decimal point.

When you work with some of these variables in your own code, you get the benefit of not having to declare anything in order to save up a spot in the memory for the value. This is something that happens automatically as soon as you assign your chosen value over to the variable, and you just need to work with the equal sign to make it happen.

As you can imagine, assigning a value with the variable is going to be easy. You just need to make sure that there is an equal sign between the value and the variable you would like to sign if over to. Some of the examples of how we would assign the variable with a value will include:

x = 12   #this is an example of an integer assignment

pi = 3.14   #this is an example of a floating point assignment

customer name = John Doe   #this is an example of a string assignment

Another option that you can do here, and that we have mentioned a little bit in this chapter already, has a variable assigned to two or more values. There are some instances when you are writing code and you will need to take two values and place them with the same variable.

To do this, you simply need to use the same procedure that we talked about above. Just make sure that you add in an equal sign to each part to help the compiler know that these are all associated with the same variable. So, you would want to write out something like for example a = b = c = 1 to show the compiler that each of these variables equals one. Or you could have 1 = b = 2 to show that there are two values to a variable.

Creating a class

One of the things that come with working in Python is that it is organized based on classes and objects. This is done to help keep things in order and ensures that the parts of the code stay where you would like them. The classes are a very distinguished part of this process, and learning how to use them, and what they are for can make a big difference.

You are able to choose your class to be anything that you would like. It is basically like a container that is meant to hold onto a lot of information, which will be the objects. You can add in as many objects as you would like to this, you just have to make sure that when someone takes a look into one of the classes, they should be able to understand why all of the parts go together.

You will find that writing out a class is not as complicated as it seems, and it can really be a great option to help you write out a lot of the various codes that you would like to handle. A good example of how you can create your own Python class will be the code below:

```
class Vehicle(object):
#constructor
def_init_(self, steering, wheels, clutch, breaks, gears):
self._steering = steering
```

```python
self._wheels = wheels
self._clutch = clutch
self._breaks =breaks
self._gears  = gears
#destructor
def_del_(self):
    print("This is destructor....")

#member functions or methods
def Display_Vehicle(self):
   print('Steering:' , self._steering)
   print('Wheels:', self._wheels)
   print('Clutch:', self._clutch)
   print('Breaks:', self._breaks)
   print('Gears:', self._gears)
#instantiate a vehicle option
myGenericVehicle = Vehicle('Power Steering', 4, 'Super
Clutch', 'Disk Breaks', 5)

myGenericVehicle.Display_Vehicle()
```

While we are at it here, take some time to open up your compiler and type in the code. This is going to give you some good practice when it comes to writing out not just classes in Python, but any of the codes that you would like to work with. You can then run the code and see what will happen when you are able to create a class of your very own.

Before you start to do any kind of coding, it is important to go through and learn some of the basics that come with that type of code. When you are able to see the different parts as you write out codes, later on, you will find that it is easier to work on those codes, and some of the stress about learning something brand new can fade away. Make sure to look out for some of these basics when we start to write out some codes later on.

Chapter 4: The Best Python Libraries to Use with Data Science

Now that we know a bit about the basics that come with the Python language, it is important that we spend some time learning the best libraries and extensions that we are able to add into the mix to make sure that Python is going to work the way that we would like for data science. The regular library that comes with Python can do a lot of amazing things, but it is not going to be able to handle all of the graphing, mathematics, and the machine learning that we need with data science.

The good news here though is that there are a few other libraries that we are able to work with that utilize Python and can help with machine learning and data science together. All of these are going to help us handle tasks in a slightly different manner so take a look at them and how they are meant to work with

Python and data science. The best libraries that can help you to get this work done will include:

NumPy and SciPy

If you want to do any kind of work with machine learning or data science with Python, you have to make sure that you work with the NumPy and the SciPy library. Both of these are going to be the basis of many of the other libraries that we are going to talk about here, which is why it is likely that when you work with data science, you are going to also add in a bit of library as well.

First, we will look at NumPy, which is going to stand for Numeric and Scientific Computation. This is a useful library because it is going to lay down some of the basic premises that we need for doing any kind of scientific computing with data science in Python. This library can also help us to get ahold of some functions that have been precompiled for us, and it is fast for handling any numerical and mathematical routine process that you would like to do.

Then there is also the Scientific Python library, which we call SciPy, that goes along with NumPy in many cases. This is the kind of library that you want to work with to add in some kind of competitive edge to what you are doing in machine learning. This happens when you work to enhance some of the useful functions for things like regression and minimization to name a few.

Matplotlib

As you are going through data science and Python, there are going to be times when you will want to work with a graph or a chart or some other kind of visual. This is going to make it easier to see the information that is found in the text, in a glance and the matplotlib will be able to make some of these graphs for you in no time.

The matplotlib extension is going to provide us with all of the parts that we need to take the info and turn it into the visualizations that you need for your data. This library is going to work with pretty much any of the different types of visualizations that you need from a histogram, bar charts, error charts, line graphs, and more.

The Scikit-Learn library

The Scikit-Learn is the library that we are going to take a look at next. This is a great one to go with when it comes to machine learning. This is because the package that comes with this library is going to provide us with a lot of machine learning algorithms and more that we can use to really get data science to work. It is going to include a lot of different parts that can ensure we analyze the informations that is fed into the algorithm in a proper manner.

One other benefit that we are going to see when it comes to this kind of library is that it is easy to distribute, which means it works well in commercial and academic kind of settings, and there are not a lot of dependencies that go with it. The interface is concise and consistent, which make it easier to work with, and you will find that the most common of the machine learning algorithms are already inside, making it easier to create some of the models you need for data science.

Pandas

The next library in Python that you want to work with to make machine learning and data science do what you would like. Pandas are going to stand for the Python Data Analysis Library, which helps us to do a lot of the work that is needed in the Python world. This is an open-sourced tool that helps us with some of the data structures that are needed to do data analysis. You can use this library to add in the right tools and data structures to make sure your data analysis is complete, and many industries like to work with this one to help out with some different processes like finance, statistics, engineering, and social science.

This Pandas library is going to be really adaptable, which makes it really great for getting a ton of work done in less time. It can also help you work with any kind of data that you are able to bring in, no matter what kind of source you are getting that info from, making it a lot easier to work with. This library is going to come with many different features that you can enjoy and some of the best ones are going to include:

1. You can use the Pandas library to help reshape the structures of your data.
2. You can use the Pandas library to label series, as well as tabular data, to help us see an automatic alignment.
3. You can use the Pandas library to help with heterogeneous indexing of the info and it is also useful when it comes to systematic labeling of the data as well.
4. You can use this library because it can hold onto the capabilities of identifying and then fixing any of the data that is missing.
5. This library provides us with the ability to load and then save data from more than one format.
6. You can easily take some of the data structures that come out of Python and NumPy and convert them into the objects that you need to Pandas objects.

TensorFlow

TensorFlow, one of the best Python libraries for data science, is a library that was released by Google Brain. It was written out mostly in the language of C++, but it is going to include some bindings in Python, so the performance is not something that you are going to need to worry about. One of the best features that comes with this library is going to be some of the flexible architecture that is found in the mix, which is going to allow the programmer to deploy it with one or more GPUs or CPUs in a desktop, mobile, or server device, while using the same API the whole time.

Not many, if any, of the other libraries that we are using in this chapter, will be able to make this kind of claim. This library is also unique in that it was developed by the Google Brain project, and it is not used by many other programmers. However, you do need to spend a bit more time to learn the API compared to some of the other libraries. In just a few minutes, you will find that it is possible to work with this TensorFlow library in order to implement the design of your network, without having to fight through the API as you do with other options.

The Keras library

If you are looking for a Python library that can handle data science and data analytics that is also easy for the user to work with, then this is the library for you. It is able to handle a lot of the different processes that come with the other libraries, but it keeps in mind the user, rather than the machine when it comes to designing the interface and the other parts that you use within this coding library. The user experience is easy, the interface is designed to only need a few clicks to get the processes done and it all comes together to make data science and machine learning as easy as possible.

This library is going to work a lot of the modules that are needed for machine learning. You can work with a module that is on its own, or you can combine together a few modules in order to get the results that you would like. There is a lot of flexibility that comes with using this kind of library, and that is one of the many reasons that so many programmers like to use it when completing work with Python data science.

These are just a few of the different libraries that you are able to use along with the Python coding language to get some of your data science and machine learning work done. These libraries all work on slightly different types of processes when it comes to data science, which is going to make them so much easier to work with overall. Take a look at each one, and see just how they can all come together to provide you with the results that you want in your data analytics project.

Chapter 5: The Basics of Jupyter and Why We Should Use It

The first library or extension that we are going to take a look at when it comes to doing some data science with the help of Python is the Jupyter extension. Jupyter, which was formally known as the Jupyter Project, is a non-profit organization that works to create computing software that is open-sourced and interactive. It was founded in 2014 as a language-agnostic version of Interactive Python and it is going to provide tools for a lot of different people, including computing professionals, data analysts, scientists, and mathematicians. It is so useful because it allows all of these professionals to write code interactively, to view the results in real-time, and then they can take the results and publish them online.

The first thing that we need to take a look at here is the Jupyter notebook. This is a useful piece of the code because it is going to be an interactive computing environment and a web server that works with Python. It is going to provide users of this product with a browser-based user interface, or UI, to make things easier. The notebooks on this library are going to be ordered lists with cells for the input and output, and each one is going to provide us with a read eval print loop, or REPL, for writing outcode and a window to show us the output that is going to come from this in real-time.

Even with this information, we may be curious as to why we would want to learn about this library at all and why we should care. It has not been able to gain the same buzz as some of the other options out there, like data science and artificial intelligence. But one thing that you may like here against some of the other things is that compared to the abstract parts that come with artificial intelligence, Jupyter is going to be very concrete. This means that it is able to handle some specific things to help with data science as well.

But without being able to bring in a lot of hype, the Jupyter Notebooks are going to revolutionize the way engineers and data scientists are going to work together. If all of the important work that we see is collaborative, the most important tools that we are going to have here will, of course, be tools for collaboration, which means that they will help us work together and become more productive.

That is basically, what Jupyter is going to be in a nutshell. It is going to be a tool that helps your team to collaborate with one another. It is built to help with writing and then sharing code and text, and this is often done within the context of one of the pages online. The code is going to run on a server, and the results can then turn it into HTML and incorporated into the page that you plan to write out.

That server can be anywhere. You may find it on your laptop, behind the firewall that you have, or on the public internet as well. Your page is important, it's going to contain all of your code, the thoughts that you have during the process, and any results that you are able to get when it comes to running the code and how you can make the right changes that are needed.

Remember in this process that code is never going to be just a code. It is going to be a big thought process, sometimes an argument, and there are times when it will show up as an experiment. This is going to be really present when we work with data analysis, but we can see this show up with almost any kind of application that we do that includes some form of coding.

When you are inside of coding, you will find that Jupyter is great because it allows you to build up to something called a lab notebook that will show your work. All of the work that you have done on that project, including the code you wrote, the data, and any results will show up here, along with any of the reasoning and explanations that you decide to write out. This will help you see what you were thinking at all of the different stages of your work, making it easier to see what changes you should make. It also helps others understand some of the reasons behind your coding decisions and the results that you are able to get.

A good way to look at Jupyter is with the definition given with IBM. According to this company, Jupyter lets you build a "computational narrative that distills data into insights." Data means nothing if you are not able to take it and turn it into some insights. If you are not able to take that informations and then explore it, discuss it, and share it with others on the team or in the business, then the data is pretty much worthless to you. Data analysis is not going to mean a lot to you if you are not able to explore and experiment with some of the results that someone else has gotten as well. And Jupyter is the tool from Python that helps us to do all of these things.

One thing that is nice about Jupyter is that we are able to take a notebook from this extension and share it. You are able to save up the work that you do, and then send it as an attachment, allowing another person of your choice to open up one of the notebooks and look through it. You can even put it on the GitHub repository and allow others to read the information as well. GitHub also takes this further and allows the notebook to become a web page that is static so that the users are able to download their own copy of the network, and any files they want to expand on the work, modify the code, inspect the results, and then see what is going to happen as a result.

Remember that Jupyter is all about collaboration, so the different ways that you can use and share the notebook is going to make a big difference in how well we can do this collaboration. Sharing of the items can be as public as you would like. You can run this on your laptop, which means that you can access it any time that you would like, but it will still remain inaccessible to anyone else who is not able to get on your computer.

You also have the choice of running this on a server that is multi-user, such as with JupyterHub, behind the firewall that your company has set up. This helps to ensure that anyone on the team is able to take a look at the notebook and see what is there makes changes, and discuss the information to see the best results in the process. This is the best way to make sure that the collaboration with your data science team is possible, without allowing everyone in the world to see the information and gather your insights as well.

While the roots of Jupyter are going to be found in Python because it evolved from one of the Notebooks of IPython, it is actually able to work with a few different languages in one. The language support is going to come to us through modular kernels, and while there is a more limited amount of kernels right now, support is coming for some more programming languages in the future. In addition to R, Python, and Julia right now, there are kernels in this notebook to help out for Haskell, Ruby, C#, Go, Java, JavaScript, and 50+ other programming languages as well.

Of course, we are going to focus mainly on how this language can be used along with the Python coding language and how we would use it to help us get more done with Python overall and data science. But it's clear to see that this Notebook has a lot of different applications, and if you need to do something in another coding language this is also possible.

The sharing process with Jupyter is going to become even easier when we combine it together with Docker. One major problem that a lot of developers are going to face in programming is making sure that all of the libraries and software that are needed to run someone else's code are present. Things like incompatibilities with versions and operating systems can make the process really stressful and it can take you several days or longer just to get the right kind of software on the computer and ready to go. But when you work with Docker and Jupyter together, this problem is going to disappear because it includes all of the parts that you need to get that notebook running.

Now, we also need to take a quick look at some of the architecture that comes with Jupyter and see some of the different parts that are important to this kind of extension. We don't need to know all of the internals at this point, but it is important to understand what's going to help you build over time. Remember, Jupyter is not just a tool, it is going to be a platform and an ecosystem that will help others build on top of what you have done. You will find that this system has three main parts and they include:

1. The front end with the notebook. This is the part that allows the programmer to come into it and edit and run the notebooks that they want. The front end here is going to be an application of JavaScript that is then delivered over to your browser, just like with other web applications. This end is going to be responsible for storing the notebook managing them in your local filesystem, and then sending it all over to the server with Jupyter.

2. The server: This is going to come in two formats. It can be either an application that is relatively

simple that can run with your laptop, or you can turn it into a server that can use more than one user. The JupyterHub is going to be one of the most widely used multi-user servers for this platform.

3. The kernel protocol. This protocol is going to allow the server a way to offload the task of running code over to a kernel that is a specific language. Jupyter is going to ship kernels for Python 2 and 3, but you can also work with kernels that come in other coding languages as well if you would like.

This architecture is simple and really flexible at the same time. You can have the option of substituting your own front end based on what you would like to do. For example, it is possible to build up a front end that is able to implement dashboards in real-time, you can use the protocol here to implement some support for the other languages that you want to work with, you can implement some customer servers to help create a new type of media as well.

There is a lot that you are able to do with the help of the Jupyter system, and making sure that you bring it on board to help with data science, especially if you are using the Python language kernels, it can help to make the process of data science and data analysis so much easier overall. You can then easily share the work that you have done and other parts with others in the company, letting others add to your work give suggestions, and more, and ensure that the project will get done the way that it should.

We can also take Jupyter and extend it out a bit. There are some options like adding extensions to the dashboard or some new widgets to the mix. For example, you can work with widgets that are more advanced and help with different tasks like creating maps and doing some of the interactive data visualizations, whether you want to do this in 2D or 3D. There is also an extension that can help us bridge together d3.js with Jupyter, which makes it easier for us to work on building web documents that are driven by the data we want to use.

The ecosystem that we can use with Jupyter is also going to include a few tools for publishing your various documents in a variety of manner. For example, nbviewer is going to be a simple tool that will make it easier for those who are not programmers to view the notebook through Jupyter. This version is going to be simple and will not run any kind of code or allow for modifications. It just takes what is considered the final version or the finished product and presents it as a web page. You can install this locally or you can work with a public service of it in order to rend any of the notebooks that are online available to view and look over when you want.

Right now, there is not just one single source that has all of the listings that we need for the tools, widgets, and extensions that come with Jupyter. But there are a lot of benefits of working with this kind of program, especially when you want to use data science and Python together as one. This means that there are quite a few developers who are working to build up new extensions and new features that can work with this kind of platform, and when you are able to put it all together, you are going to find that your results will be amazing.

It is estimated that in the future we will be able to use Jupyter even more than we do now. This project is already working to do some real-time collaboration with the notebooks, such as allowing more than one user to be on and editing a notebook at the same time. There is also a dynamic collaboration that is going on with a few online platforms, including Google Docs, and it is certain that Jupyter is going to come on as well.

Jupyter has become a standard in the industry when it comes to data analysis and scientific research, which is going to make it the perfect companion to work with when it comes to data science. It is going to package together with the argument and the computation together, which allows us to build up a computational narrative. In addition, some of the other things that Jupyter is going to help you do will include:

1. Allows you to take the narratives that you have and publish them in a lot of different formats, including slide decks and even online notebooks of your choice.

2. It is going to support a lot of the different languages out there for coding. We are going to focus on Python with this one, but there are a lot of other popular programming languages that have kernels that work well with this extension.

3. It is going to help simplify some of the problems that come with distributing software that is working to your associates and other teammates.

There are also a lot of different tools that are going to come in with Jupyter to help you with the three things listed above. The analytics platforms and the different IDE's are going to be the best ones to use though. You need to search through the different tools and options that come with Jupyter to see exactly how you would be able to use this, along with the Python language, to get some of your data science work done.

Chapter 6: Working with Anaconda in Python

The next package that we need to take a look at when we want to complete some work with data science and Python is the Anaconda package. This is going to help you to get a lot of different things done and can bring in some capabilities that you may not be able to get with Jupyter. There are actually a lot of different options that you are able to work with when it comes to Python Packages, and having a good understanding of how these work, and how they will go together, can make a big difference in the coding that you can do.

There is a lot that we are able to do with Python all on its own, but it is not necessarily set up to handle computational modes or any of the scientific computing that you need to do with any data science projects. This doesn't mean that you have to miss out on the ease of use or the power that comes with Python, it simply means that we need to add on some additional libraries and packages, ones that are designed to work with Python, in order to see the results.

There are a ton of different packages that you are able to add on to Python to work with scientific computing and some of the other things that we want to do with data science. But some of the major ones that we need to consider, along with anaconda will include:

1. NumPy This is for Numeric Python and it is going to help us with linear algebra and matrices.
2. SciPy: This is for scientific Python and it is used for many of the numerical routines that we have.
3. Matplotlib: This is a plotting library that helps us take our data and create a plot with it.
4. SymPy: This one stands for Symbolic Python and it handles all of the symbolic computations
5. PyTest: This one is for Python Testing and it comes in use when we want to code our own testing framework.

With this in mind, we need to focus on what Anaconda Python is all about, and why it is useful to help us with some of the different projects that we are going to work on with data science. Together, along with some of the other Python packages and tools like editors, the distribution that you get with Python is going to include the Python interpreter. And Anaconda is going to be one out of several of the options you have for the distribution of Python.

Anaconda is a relatively new distribution that works with both the R coding language and the Python coding language. In particular, it is going to be seen as a data science package, making it perfect to use with the data analysis that we have been talking about. It was formally known as the Continuum Analytics, but now it is rebranded as something new and comes with over 100 packages that a programmer can download and use along with Python.

This work environment, which is what Anaconda is all about, is something that a programmer is able to use with Python in order to handle a variety of tasks including machine learning, statistical analysis, data science, and even scientific computing. One of the most popular and latest versions of this work environment was released in October of 2017, and it is Anaconda 5.0.1. This was a helpful release to go with because it was meant to address some of the minor bugs that had shown up in the other versions, and had some other features that are useful for programming and data science work, such as updated support for the R coding language. None of these were features that we were able to get until recently.

While Anaconda is going to be a package manager, we can also use it as a type of environment manager. It is also going to be a distribution of Python, a collection of packages that are open-sourced, and it has many different Python and R data science packages that you are able to choose from. All of this comes together to help you use either the Python or the R coding language to get things done with data science, and can make the data analysis that you want to complete from earlier so much easier.

This now brings up the question of why you would want to use the Anaconda environment along with Python. There are a lot of features that you can use with Anaconda, but it is an added extension that you have to download and put in. some programmers decide that they are just as happy with some of the regular Python environments that come with the language, and that is just fine as well.

However, some of those people who like to spend time doing data science work and don't consider themselves as full time developers; can find that the Anaconda program is going to be helpful. This environment is going to be useful because it takes some of the common problems or work that you need to handle, and can really help to simplify it. As someone who may be just starting out with programming, or who is not familiar with all of the things that Python can do with data science, adding in the Anaconda package, and all that it entails, can make things easier.

When you are using the Anaconda program, you will find that it can help you out with a few different issues. Some of the things that the Anaconda package is able to assist with will include:

1. Helping us to install Python on more than one platform if that is how we intend to use it.
2. Separating out some of the various environments that we may be used with Python at the same time.

3. Dealing with the issues that come up when we don't hold onto the right privileges all the time,
4. Getting up and making sure that specific libraries and packages are running the way that they should.

Like many of the other libraries that you may work with on Python and for data science, you are able to get ahold of a free version of Anaconda. This is nice because it means that you can just take a bit of time to download it, and then it is ready to use for all of your data science needs. There are some third parties extensions that you may want to use as well that will cost, but the basic parts of both Python and the Anaconda environment are free for you and other programmers to use.

You are able to get the free version of the Anaconda distribution community edition from the main website for Anaconda. If you would like too with one of the enterprise editions, which works better for the company and professional use, then you will not be able to download this version online. You will need to get ahold of the Anaconda sales team in order to get the professional support to download this.

Conda is going to work pretty easily and it will treat Python the same way as if does in any of the other packages that you have. This is useful because it helps us to manage and then update many different installations based on what we want to see happen. You can quickly download this extension (the amount of time is going to vary based on the speed of your internet and your operating system), and then you are able to get going on a project in no time.

The default that is going to support Anaconda is Python 2.7 or 3.6 depending on the installer that you went through and used in the beginning. If you would like though Anaconda is also going to be able to support versions 3.4 and 3.5 of Python so if those are the ones that you would like to spend your time on, the Anaconda environment will work there as well.

Anaconda is one of the choices that you can make when it comes to creating a good environment to do some of your data science work with. This is even better when you need to combine together some of the R coding languages. This environment does have the capabilities to work with artificial intelligence and machine learning, which is going to make it perfect when you need to create a model or some algorithms that can handle your data analysis when you get to that point.

Remember earlier we talked about how important the analysis part of the field of data science is. This happens after the data scientist has had some time to go through and collect the info that they would like to use, and then after they have been able to clean off that data. Then Python, with the help of some tools like Anaconda and the other packages and extensions that we talked about at the beginning of the chapter will be able to come together and help us create the right package and the right algorithm to handle it all for us.

Anaconda is one of the environment, or packages, that we are able to bring into the mix to help solve some of the data science problems that we may be facing. It has a lot of the other parts that we need to put together to help with this, and will make sure that we can create models and any kind of algorithm, or group of algorithms that are needed to take care of your data analysis and to ensure that you are actually able to see some of the results and insights that you need out of your data.

Chapter 7: The Basics of the Pandas Library

The next library that we are going to spend some time on is the Pandas library. This is a great one that is always included when we look at data science, and because it works with the Python language, we know that we will see some powerful coding that is easy to get started with. With this in mind, let us take a look at some of the things that we can come to expect when we work with the Pandas library.

To start, pandas is going to be a package from Python that is open-sourced and can provide us with a lot of different tools when it comes to completing our data analysis. This package also includes a few different structures that we are able to learn about and bring out for a variety of tasks that deal with data manipulation. For someone who wants to sort through a lot of data in a quick and orderly fashion to find out the insights and predictions that are inside, the Pandas library is the best one to work with.

In addition to some of the tasks that we outlined above, Pandas is also going to bring out a lot of different methods that programmers can invoke for helping with the data analysis. This is always a good thing when we are working on things like data science and a variety of problems that machine learning is able to help us solve along the way.

While we are here, we need to take a look at some of the advantages that come with using the Pandas library over some of the others. This library may not be the one that you want to use instead of some of the others, but it is definitely one that you should consider learning about and keeping in your toolbox any time that you want to do some data analysis or work with data science in some shape or form. Some of the different advantages that you will notice with the Pandas library will include:

1. It is going to take the info that you have and present it in a manner that is suitable for analyzing the large amounts of data that you have. This data analysis is going to be completed in Pandas with the use of the DataFrame and the Series data structures.

2. You will find that the Pandas package is going to come with many methods to help us filter through

our info in a convenient manner while seeing some great results.

3. Pandas also come with a variety of utilities that are going to help us when it is time to perform the input and output operations in a way that is quick and seamless. In addition, Pandas is able to read data that comes in a variety of formats, which is very important in data science, such as Excel, TSV, and CSV to name a few.

You will find that Pandas is really going to change up the game and how you do some coding when it comes to analyzing the data a company has with Python. In fact, it is often the most used, and the most preferred tool in data wrangling and munging (we will look at how to do this more in the next chapter) in the Python language and elsewhere as well. Pandas are going to be free to use and open source and were meant to be used by anyone who is looking to handle the data they have in a safe, fast, and effective manner.

There are a lot of other libraries that are out there, but you will find that a lot of companies and individuals are going to love working with Pandas. One thing that is really cool about Pandas is that it is able to take info, whether it is from an SQL database, a TSV file or even a CSV file, and then it will take that information and create it into a Python object. This is going to be changed over to columns and rows and will be called a data frame, one that will look very similar to a table that we are going to see in other software that is statistical.

If you have worked with R in the past, then the objects are going to share a lot of similarities to R as well. And these objects are going to be easier to work with when you want to do work and you don't want to worry about dictionaries or lists for loops or list comprehension. Remember that we talked earlier about how loops can be nice in Python, but you will find that when it comes to data analysis, these loops can be clunky, take up a lot of space, and just take too long to handle. Working with this kind of coding language will help you to get things done without all of the mess along the way.

For the most part, it is going to be best if you are able to download the Pandas library at the same time that you download Python. This makes it easier to work with and will save you sometime later. But if you already have Python on your computer and later decide that you want to work with Pandas as well, then this is not a problem. Take some time now to find the pandas library on its official page and follow the steps that are needed to download it on the operating system of your choice.

Once you have had some time to download the Pandas library, it is time to actually learn how this one works and some of the different things that you are able to do to get it to work for you. The Pandas library is a lot of fun because it has a ton of capabilities that are on it, and learning what these are and how to work with them is going to make it easier to complete some of your own data analysis in the process.

At this point, the first thing that we need to focus on is the steps that we can take to load up any data, and even save it before it can be run through with some of the algorithms that come with Pandas. When it is time to work with this library from Python in order to take all of that data you have collected and then learn something from it and gain insights, we have to keep in mind that there are three methods that we can use with this. These three methods are going to include the following:

1. You can convert a NumPy array, a Python list or a Python dictionary over to the data frame that is available with Pandas.

2. You can open up a local file that is found on your computer with the help of Pandas. This is often going to be something like a CSV file, but it is possible that it could be something else like Excel or a delimited text file in some cases.

3. You can also choose to use this in order to open up a file or another database that are remote, including a JSON or CSV that is located on a website through a URL or you can have the program read through it on a database or a table that is from SQL.

Now, as you go through with these three steps, we have to remember that there are actually a couple of commands that will show up for each one, and it depends on which method you go with what command you will choose. However, one thing that all three shares in common are that the command they use to open up a info file will be the same. The command that you need to use to open up your info file, regardless of the method above that you choose to use will include:

Pd.red_filetype()

Like we talked about a bit earlier on, and throughout this guidebook, there are a few file types that you are able to use and see results with when writing in Python. And you get the control of choosing which one is the best for your project. So, when working on the code above, you would just need to replace the part that says "filetype" with the actual type of file that you would like to use. You also need to make sure that you add in the name of your file, the path, or another location to help the program pull it up and know what it is doing.

You will find that while you work in the Pandas library, there are also a ton of arguments that you are able to choose from and to know what all of these mean and how to pull up each one at the right time is going to be a big challenge. To save some time, and to not overwhelm you with just how many options there are, we are going to focus on just the ones that are the most important for our project, the ones that can help us with a good info analysis, and leave the rest alone for now.

With this idea in mind, we are going to start out by learning how we can convert one of the objects that we are already using in Python, whether this is a list or a dictionary or something else, over to the pandas' library so we can actually use it for our needs. The command that we are able to use to make that conversion happen is going to include:

Pd.InfoFrame()

With the code above, the part that goes inside of the parenthesis is where we are able to specify out the different object, and sometimes the different objects, that are being created inside that info frame. This is the command that will bring out a few arguments, and you can choose which ones of those you want to work with here as well.

In addition to helping out with some of the tasks that we just listed out, we can also use Pandas to help us save that info frame, so we can pull it up and do more work later on, or if we are working with more than one type of file. This is nice because Pandas is going to save tables that come in many different formats, whether that is CSV, Excel, SQL, or JSON. The general code that we need to use to help us not only work on the framework that we are currently on, but to make sure that we can save it as well will include the following:

Df_to.filetype(filename)

When we get to this point, you should see that the info is already loaded up, so now we need to take this a step further and look at some of the inspecting that can be done with this as well. To start this, we need to take a look at the frame of the info and see whether or not it is able to match up with what we expect or want it to. To help us do this, we just need to run the name of the info frame we are choosing to bring up the entire table, but we can limit this a bit more and get more control by only getting a certain amount of the table to show up based on what we want to look at.

For example, to help us just get the first n amount of rows (you can decide how many rows this ends up being), you would just need to use the function of df.heat(n). Alternatively, if your goal was to work with the n number of rows that are last in the table, you would need to write out the code df.tail(n). The df.shape is going to help if you want to work with the number of columns and rows that show up, and if you would like to gather up some of the information that is there about the info type, memory or the index, the only code that you will need to use to make this happen is df.info().

Then you can also take over the command of: s.value_counts(dropna=False) and this one allows us to view some of the unique values and counts for the series, such as if you would like to work with just one, and sometimes a few, columns. A useful command that you may want to learn as well is going to be the df.describe() function. This one is going to help you out by inputting some of the summary statistics that come with the numerical columns. It is also possible for you to get the statistics on the entire info frame or a series.

To help us make a bit more sense out of what we are doing here, and what it all means, we need to look at a few of the different commands that you are able to use in Pandas that are going to help us view and inspect the info we have. These include:

1. df.mean(). This function is going to help us get the mean of all our columns.
2. df.corr() This function is going to return the correlation between all of the columns that we have in the frame of info.
3. Df.count(): This function is going to help us return the number of non-null values in each of the frames of info based on the columns.
4. Df.max(). The function is going to return the highest value in each of the columns.
5. Df.min(). This function is going to return the lowest value that is found in each of the columns that you have.
6. Df.median(). This is going to be the function that you can use when you want to look at each column and figure out the median.
7. Df.std(). This function is going to be the one that you would use in order to look at each of the columns and then find the standard deviation that comes with it.

Another cool thing that we are able to do when working on the Pandas library is that we are able to join together and combine different parts. This is a basic command in Python, so learning how to do it from the beginning can make a big difference. But it is so important for helping us to combine or join the frames of info, or to help out with combining or joining the rows and columns that we want. There are three main commands that can come into play to make all of this happen, the following are going to include:

1. Dfl.appent(df2). This one is going to add in the rows of df1 to the end of df2. You need to make sure that the columns are going to be identical in the process.

2. Df.concat([df1, df2], axis=1). This command is going to add in the columns that you have in df1 to the end of what is there with df2. You want to make sure that you have the rows added together identical.

3. Dfl.oin(df2, on=col1, hot='inner'). This is going to be an SQL style join the columns in the df1 with the columns on df2 where the rows for col have identical values how can be equal to one of left, right, inner, and outer.

There is so much that we are able to do when it comes to the Pandas library, and that is one of the reasons why it is such a popular option to go with. Many companies who want to work with info science are also going to be willing to add on the Pandas extension because it helps them to do a bit more with info science, and the coding is often simple thanks to the Python language that runs along with it.

The commands that we looked at in this chapter are going to be some of the basic ones with Python and with Pandas, but they are meant to help us learn a bit more about this language, and all of the things that we can do with the Pandas library when it comes to Python and to the info science work that we would like to complete. There is a lot of power that comes with the Pandas library, and being able to put all of this together, and use some of the algorithms and models that come with this library can make our info analysis so much better.

The work that we did in this chapter is a great introduction to what we are able to do with the Pandas library, but this is just the beginning. You will find that when you work with Pandas to help out with your info analysis, you are going to see some great results, and will be able to really write out some strong models and codes that help not only to bring in the info that your company needs, but to provide you with the predictions and insights that are needed as well so your business can be moved to the future.

Chapter 8: What is WinPython and How Can We Use It?

The next kind of library that we are going to work with is the WinPython library. This is going to be a method that allows us to use the Python program well on a Windows computer, without having any cross issues between the two. Windows has its own coding language, so it does not always like to work with other coding languages. You can do it, but many programmers like to have a separate kind of environment to help them do the coding, without any interference from the Windows program in the process.

Because of this, there is not a distribution for Python that is considered standard. This is where WinPython is going to come into play. This is a complete development environment that is portable and is going to include some of the most important scientific and info science libraries including NumPy and SciPy on them. It is even going to take this a bit further and will include an IDE for Python, namely Spyder here, along with a creative control system of Mercuria, and Qt tools that make it easier to work with the development of GUI with any program that you would like.

While there are a lot of neat features that come with this program, and you are able to find a lot to love when coding in this language, one of the things that a lot of coders and programmers like when they are working with this system is that they can use the WinPython Package Manager or WPPM. This WPPM is going to allow the programmer to install any packages that they want with the standard installers. These will be either the easy_install, the pip, or the distutils standard installers.

The latter one of these is going to be the most interesting because it is going to include some dependencies that are binary, which means that we are not going to need to use a compiler that can work with C or C++. For those who are not comfortable with using other coding languages outside of Python, or who don't have the time to learn C or C++ along with Python, having this kind of package can make life a little bit easier.

If scientific computing is going to be your thing, and you want to be able to handle some of the different parts that come with info science and completing info analysis then this is one of the best libraries that you can work with. This is especially when it comes to doing some work with Python and info science on a Windows computer.

Another interesting feature that you may see with using this version of Python is that it does provide us with the possibility of converting our portable distribution over into a more conventional kind of installation in Python on Windows, simply by adding in a few keys to the registry that we are using. You can also do this step through the Control Panel of WinPython. You can also work with a few different versions of Python to make all of this happen.

There are several different alternatives that you are able to use when it is time to install Python on a computer that has Windows. However, if you plan to work with Python in order to do info science, scientific work, or even mathematics and statistics, then you are going to need to work with some of the scientific packages as well. These will include some of the packages like OpenCV, Matplotlib, SciPy, and NumPy.

When you are working with these scientific packages through Python, you will often have to work with one option of installing them on a Windows computer. This is going to result in you configuring Windows PATH, and then installing several of the Microsoft Visual C++ versions, and the more compiling that you end up doing, the more it is going to cause confusion and just complicate things for us.

Of course, no one wants to work with these processes and have things more complicated than they need to be. Info science and the info analysis is already too complicated, so why would we want to make this more difficult to handle overall rather than just dealing with it in a simple manner. This is where WinPython is going to come into play to help us see some good results in the process while simplifying the process that we are doing.

WinPython is going to be a basic standalone version of Python that you are able to use in order to bring in much of the packages, environments, and tools that you need. All of these are going to be installed on the computer with this extension, and they will be ready to use all in one. Plus you can use Python and all of its libraries and extensions without having to mess with the Windows PATH at all. In addition, you are able to install as many versions of this program as you would like, and it comes in both Python 2 and Python 3.

For many people, working with the Windows operating system is one of the best options to help ensure that we are going to be able to get the work done. But since Windows is going to have its own coding language already installed, it is sometimes difficult to add in some Python and see the results that you would like. This makes it more complicated to get all of the libraries on and ready to go with this operating system without some kind of interference showing up in the process.

This is exactly what the WinPython extension is going to help us with. It is basically a version of Python that is designed to work with the Windows operating system. You are able to download this onto your system and have all of the applications, libraries and tools that you need to handle info science and info analysis, without it interfering with the Windows operating system at all. It will work on its own, without any issues with the operating system or the language that comes with Windows.

If you are already planning on working with info science when you get started, and you are going to use a Windows operating system, then it is probably a good idea to install this onto your system and use it. It can make it a lot easier with your coding and if nothing else, it ensures that you have all of the different parts of the code that you need and all of the extensions and libraries that are needed in one place.

There are a number of benefits that come with using WinPython for all of your needs. Remember here that it is a Python-based environment that works on some of the technical and scientific aspects that you would like to see when working in info science. Some of the different things that you are going to enjoy when it comes to working with this kind of library include:

1. It has been designed for the info scientist in mind and also works well for scientists and educators. This is because it comes along with some of the other libraries that you need for this process including Pandas, Matplotlib, SymPy, SciPy, and NumPy.

a. This is going to be an interactive environment that includes info processing and visualization. It is going to rely on Python along with a few of the other extensions that we have included in this guidebook.

b. It can also work with a compiler that is out of the box for Python 3.4 and it is fully integrated with Numba! and Cython.

c. It has a few different connectors that work the best for advanced users.

2. The library is portable. This extension is going to run out of the box on any computer that has the Windows 8 operating system or newer. Your Jupyter Notebook, if you choose to work with this environment, is going to require that you have a recent browser so keep this in mind.

a. You are able to move the folder for WinPython to any location that you would like with most of the settings for the application. This means that you can put it anywhere you would like whether on a USB drive, your network, or on a local drive on the computer.

3. WinPython is really flexible. You are able to install as many of these distributions as you would like, even on the same machine. Each one of these is going to be self-consistent and isolated so you won't have to worry about them getting in the way or causing any problems with your system.

   a. These installations can even go further and be different versions of Python and different architectures as well.

4. This environment is going to be more customizable. This integrated package manager, or WPPM, will help to install, uninstall, or upgrading the different packages that you have with Python.

   a. The programmer is even able to install or upgrade packages using the pip from the WinPython command prompt to make installing and using programs so much easier than before.

   b. This comes with the configuration file that is helpful because it makes it easier to set the variables for the environment at runtime as well.

You will find as you work through this process, this environment is going to provide you something that is a bit different than what we see with the other distributions of Python. This can make it so much easier to use this version of the program, rather than some of the other versions of libraries, which will provide you with some of the info science help that you would like.

First, you will notice that this environment can be on your computer without being invasive. WinPython is able to live entirely with its own directory. This means that it does not need to go through an installation on your operating system. This takes less room on your computer, makes the program easier to move around, and can save us a lot of space as well.

Another benefit here, or something unique about WinPython that you will enjoy is that it is really customizable. You are able to add any kind of customization that you would like to this program, which helps to make it easier to use for all of your info science needs. It is going to allow us to add in the missing packages, zip up the directory here, and you can then even give it off to students or other members of the team to finish off the project.

And finally, another thing that makes this environment more unique compared to some of the others is that you are able to create one of your own versions. There is a kit for WinPython that is able to create the work for you. The WinPython creator kit is available for any programmer who would like to be able to create their own version of this for their own needs.

You will find that this WinPython is going to be an application that is really portable so the user has to remember that there is not going to be any kind of integration into the Windows explorer when you go through the process of installing the whole thing. However, the control panel that comes with this does help with this problem because it is going to help you to register your distribution with Windows so that the two programs are able to work with one another.

There are a few reasons why you would want to register the installation of WinPython with Windows, rather than just leaving things the way they are and having the Windows operating system, and this installation work separately. Some of the things that will happen when you register the installation of WinPython on your computer include:

1. You will be able to associate some of your file extensions, including .pyo, pyc, and .py over to the interpreter of Python.
2. It can help you to register some of the icons that come with Python back to the Windows Explorer.
3. It helps you to add in some context menu entries Edit with IDLE and Edit with Spyder for some of the .py files that you are working on.
4. It will help you to register WinPython as a standard Python distribution. This is going to be a standard Python Windows installer so that you can see the WinPython in your Windows registry.

This is exactly the same thing that you would see happening when you use the official installer for Python, and how it would react to the machine that you are using it on whether that is with Windows or another operating system. This means that with the steps above, and making sure that you register the environment in with Windows you are able to have it both ways and enjoy the benefits of this program.

As you can see, there are a lot of benefits that we are able to find when it is time to work with the Python language and see some great results in the process. You will find that WinPython is a great option to add in when you are working with info science and the world of Python. You will be able to add this onto any computer you would like to use that has a Windows operating system and that you would like to run Python with, and see some great results in the process. Make sure to check out this extension to see what you are able to do when it comes to working with the WinPython program.

Chapter 9: Common Tasks to Do in Info Science

When it comes to working on info science, there are going to be many different tasks that you are able to focus on. Companies have found that they are able to work with info science in many different ways, and it has made their decision-making and other common tasks so much easier than before. Info science is able to take a lot of info that the company has collected over time and then helps the company to use that data to make decisions, to know what is going to happen in the future, and more. Some of the tasks that data science is commonly used for will include:

Helps us to get through a lot of data.

One of the main reasons that companies like to work with data science is because this process is going to help them search through and sort out a lot of data all at once. Many businesses are going to just add it into their process to gather up data from a variety of sources, and then this data, due to the different sources, is going to come in a variety of formats. This means that for us to be successful, we need to come up with a way to go through all of this data to see what is inside. This is exactly what data science is going to help us out with.

Companies who gather up this different kind of data will work to gather it up from many sources overall. You may find this data from some of your social media sites from asking questions in surveys, from doing research studies, from some third party research that others have done.

While the company is in the process of collecting all of this data, which is the first step to the process of data science, it is still important to make sure that we are gathering good information, information that actually tells us a good deal about our customers, about the industry, about the competition and so much more. In some cases, you will be able to use this data to not only provide you with some good insights on all of the things above, but it can help you to make smart predictions about the future.

In the past, a company may not have spent so much time gathering all of this industry, or even about their customers. Most companies in the past were smaller and did not need to do all of this work in order to see results. They just had to have good standing in their area and present a high-quality product. But the world of business has changed, and with all of the competition out there and the choices for customers to choose from, it is important to do this kind of data analysis in order to learn how you can stand out from others, and even make a profit.

While it is common to wonder if it is even worth the time and effort to hire a data scientist to help with the algorithms and to sift through all of that data, think about the information and insights you are missing out on in the meantime. And think about how much longer it would take to have someone manually go through all of the information, rather than having a professional with some good algorithms do the work.

Helps with making some predictions.

Being able to make some predictions about the future is often seen as the best way for a company to be prepared for what might happen to them in the future, and to ensure that you can keep that business running strong, even when there are some bad times going on in the industry. The data that a company is going to be able to collect through the process of data science and the insights that are going to show themselves when you work with the right model or algorithm is going to go a long way in making predictions for your company.

Let's look at an example of how this is going to work. Let's say that you are looking at a few weather models and charts and you see that this year the winter is predicted to be really cold. You want to figure out what this is going to mean for some of the sales that your business has, whether you should increase or decrease inventory, and how you should handle some of your staffing needs.

As you are looking through some of the data about sales in the past, you start to notice that on other winters that were similar to this one, the sales in your stores went up. For example, maybe you sell winter coats or video games and people like to purchase these to keep warm or to have something to do during the cold rather than being outside.

With this kind of thing in mind, and after checking through with more than one model to make sure that this prediction is accurate, it is time to make some plans on how to handle the winter. Maybe because it is going to be so cold, and based on how your sales have done on other similar winters, you keep more inventory on hand or you expand out your hours to handle the extra customers. And you want to make sure that you have enough employees on hand to keep up with the extra customers that come in as well.

But this can go the opposite way as well. Maybe the weather predictions are telling us that the winter is going to be warm, and this usually means, based on your past data that your sales are going to go down. You may take the opposite approach and limit the stock that you keep on hand, be careful about how many people you hire, and even consider limiting your hours to just when you are going to be the busiest.

In both of these scenarios, you are able to get ahold of information about the season and then compare how your sales have done in other similar years. The right model or algorithm that you work with is going to ensure that you will see the right information, and then you can plan out how your business will run from all of this information.

Can give you a good idea of the best products to send to market

Depending on how you plan on using the data, it is possible to use some of the processes of data science to give you an idea of what products are the best to produce. Many companies who have decided that data science is the best option for them will decide to use the data life cycle in order to figure out the best products to offer onto the market next. This process does take a bit longer because it is necessary to collect the data and then sort through it all over time, it is going to ensure that when the product is all finished, it is going to be accepted on the market and do well.

When it comes to the traditional process of creating and then selling a product, there is a good chance of risk that comes with it all. You may know quite a bit about the business world, and sometimes there are just those ideas that we instantly know will be a great hit. But there is always going to be a big risk for making and selling these products without the right market research and more into it. Whole companies have gone under because of this risk. With all of the time, money, and talent that can go into a product over the years before you even release it, it is too risky to go out in our modern world and release a product without proper planning along the way.

The good news is that if we work with data science and all of the methods that come with it, it is possible to reduce some of the risks that come with these products. You have to take the right steps to gather up the information, and it is never a good idea to make assumptions about this either. But if data science is there, you know that all business decisions you make, even ones that have to do with product development are backed up with data, and you know they will do well on the market before you even send them out.

Improve how much customer satisfaction is present.

Another way that a business is able to work with data science is to improve customer satisfaction. Every company knows that their success is going to hinge on how much their customers are going to enjoy the product and the service, and whether they come back or not. If you do not provide a good product or your employees are not providing the kind of assistance that the customer wants, then you are going to lose them, and it is hard to get them back. Customer satisfaction is going to be the key to a successful business.

There are many methods that you are able to work with when it comes to data science in order to understand your customer better, and you can use this process to help learn what the customer is looking for when they use your business. Surveys are a popular option to see what the customer liked about the store or what brought them there in the first place. Following social media, doing research groups and more can provide you with a lot of insights that you were not expecting.

All of the information that you can gather through this process is going to come together to make it easier for us to know our customer, to provide a great service or product, and learn some of the new methods that come into play to make our customers happy. Often this is where we are going to learn about the best products to offer, and it can be a great place to explore some of the outliers in the information to see if there is a great new market or industry that we can work with to reach more customers.

Saves the company a lot of money

Many times companies are going to work with data science because it is an easy way for them to learn where they can effectively cut costs and improve their bottom line. Every business wants to be able to save money where they can and increase their bottom line, but sometimes without the insights that data science can provide, this is hard to even get started with.

When we talk about cutting down on costs though, our goal is not to cut down and make a cheaper product or cut corners and make something that no one wants to buy or something that is not safe to work with. Our goal with this one instead is more about finding the places where waste is going on, and was improving that area will not cause any negative effects on the product or service. In fact, often we are able to improve the product or service when we do take steps to reduce waste.

An example of this would be when a company works with data science to figure out where some of the production lulls are going to show up, and then determine where you can reduce the length of these lulls. Data analysis and data science have, in some cases, been able to help a company learn when a machine is going to upgrade or when it needs a new part. Then the company is able to schedule this at night time or other times that are down to reduce the amount of time that is wasted repairing the item during the regular working hours.

Sometimes this process is going to be used to learn the best ways to make your production work and how to shorten the assembly line and save some time, while making the job easier for the employees, and so much more in the process. As a business owner, you will find that data science is going to make it easier for the business to look at the best ways to save money and they won't have to cut around any corners or do things that make the customers leave without looking back.

This is why data science is the best solution for pretty much any business, no matter what industry to see an increase in their profits and bottom line, while still beating out the competition with products that are high quality and that your customers actually want to purchase.

Data science is going to come through and help us out with many of the processes that we need to make our business run in a smooth and controlled manner. And when you are able to make all of these parts come together, you will find that the data science process is able to make your business stronger, helps you to see happier customers, the increase of the profits that you make, and can cut out a lot of waste. All of these are going to be critical when it comes to having and running a successful business.

Chapter 10: Different Data Types to Work With

Big data and data science is something that is really on the mind of almost every business owner. Despite this fact though, not everyone is going to clearly understand that not all of the data in play is the same, and not all of these business owners are going to have a clear vision of the types of applications and the different technologies that are available through data science. Machine learning, artificial intelligence, and data science are seen as the same things sometimes, but it is important to come in here with an understanding that not all data is the same, which helps us to see that not all of the techniques that are used with data science are going to be the same either.

Structured data

The first type of data that we are going to take a look at is known as structured data. This is going to be any kind of data that has been organized into a formatted repository, usually a database of some kind so that the various elements that come with this can be addressable for more effective processing and analysis overall.

A data structure is going to be the repository that can help to organize the information that we are using for this purpose. For example, in a database, each field is going to be left as discrete and its information can be retrieved either separately or along with the data from some other fields, based on what you would like to see done. The power of the database is its ability to make the data comprehensive so that it provides you with the useful information that you are looking for.

Structured data is going to differ from some of the other types of data because of how it is formulated and how we are planning on using it. This data is often easier to read through and can make training some of the sets of data that we want to use later on, but it is often going to be more expensive and takes longer to collect so we need to keep this in mind.

Unstructured data

The second type of data that we are going to take a look at is known as unstructured data. This is the type that will not follow with a specified format for big data. If 20 percent of the data that you have available is structured, then the other 80 percent will fall into this category. This kind of data is the kind that you are most likely to encounter because it is easier to get and costs less, but you will need to go through some extra steps to learn about this data and to get it organized for your algorithms.

You will find that this kind of data is everywhere. In fact, most individuals and companies are going to conduct their lives with this kind of data. This data, just like what we see with structured data, is going to be either human-generated or machine-generated. There are a lot of different examples when it comes to working with unstructured data that has been generated by a machine. Some of these will include:

1. Images from satellites: This is going to include data about the weather or the info that governments can capture in their satellite surveillance imagery.
2. Scientific data. This could include things like high energy physics, atmospheric data, and seismic imagery.
3. Video and photography: This could be things like traffic video and security in some cases.
4. Radar: This would include what we find with the weather as well as vehicular and meteorological profiles.

In addition to these machine-generated forms of unstructured data, it is possible that we can find some of the unstructured data that fits in with human-generated forms. Some of the examples of human-generated unstructured data will include the following:

1. Text that is internal to just your company. This could include things like emails the results of a survey, logs, and the text inside of documents.
2. Social media data. Companies are always turning to social media to reach their customers, and they can also generate a lot of data from these platforms, no matter which one is used.
3. Mobile data. As the world is moving more to their phones and other mobile devices, it makes sense

that we can use data including information on the location of the individual and their text messages.

4. Website content: This would come to form any site that is going to deliver content that is unstructured. Some examples of this will include Instagram Flickr, and YouTube.

Because there is so much of this data, and it is less expensive to gather compared to the structured data, we will find that this is going to take up quite a bit of the data equation. And the uses that we are able to come up with this unstructured data are expanding all of the time. On just the side of the text on its own, text analytics can be used to help analyze the unstructured text and to help extract the data that is relevant while transforming that data into information that is more structured and can be used in a variety of ways.

Which type of data is the best?

The next thing that we need to consider is what type of data, whether structured or unstructured, is the best one for you to use. This is often going to depend on what your overall project is about, and how high quality the data is to make the model work the way that you would like.

Usually, the structured data is going to be the type that is considered the best. This is because this data is going to come from higher quality sources compared to the others, and it is often labeled, which can help our algorithm or our model learn faster than before. This kind of data is going to require less work on the side of programming because you are able to get the machine learning or the artificial intelligence models that you want to work with.

However, there are some downsides to using this kind of data. While it can make training easier and is often considered to be of higher quality than the unstructured data, this kind of data is harder to get ahold of. Since it comes with labels and is easier to fit into a table, it takes longer to collect. Sometimes this is fine and can work for a business. But for those who need to make quick decisions right now looking for a bunch of structured data can be too time-consuming for them to finish.

Another disadvantage here is the cost. Having someone go out and search for all of the structured data that you need to make your model work well, and you do need quite a bit of data, can be expensive. Often businesses do not have the resources to complete a whole model with just structured data, and so they have to make some compromises. The structured data may be good and can make life easier, but businesses often have to weigh the benefit against the cost factor to determine the best option for them.

Then there is the unstructured data. This is going to be a little bit different than what we will see with the structured data, and often it will rely more on things like images and videos, and a lot of the information from social media will count under this category as well. This kind is considered lower quality compared to some of the text files that you can get, or the other categories that fit with structured data, but it still has a lot of value, and many businesses do focus on using this.

To start, gathering the unstructured data is usually faster and you can gather a large amount in much less time than what we can do with the structured data. This makes it easier to get the amount of info that is needed to handle our analysis and the algorithms that we want to do. And with the growth of social media and all of the data that a company is able to gather from there on a daily basis, it makes sense that more businesses are relying on this unstructured data to help them out.

In addition, this unstructured data costs less than what we see with the structured data. Since this is not going to come with any labels already on it, and we don't have to spend so much time searching for it, the unstructured data is easier to handle, and will not cost us as much to find and implement it into the models. And just because it is lower quality than the structured data, that doesn't mean that it is worthless. Businesses will be able to benefit quite a bit from using this unstructured data in their models to help them make decisions and learn some valuable insights.

For many businesses, working with a combination of the structured and the unstructured data is a lot easier. This helps them to get some of the higher quality in there, while still keeping their costs down as much as possible. You will be able to add in some quality control to the models that you are creating in Python, while still ensuring that you can gather the amount of data that you need to make the algorithm work. And all of this without blowing your budget on just the data, before anything else is even done.

Having the right kind of data is going to be so important when it comes to working with data science. You want to pick out data that is high quality, but the amount of data can also be important when you need to train up a new model or algorithm to run the way that you want. Having a nice balance between the structured and the unstructured data is going to be so important to ensure that we see this workout and that all of the goals of the data analysis can be met in a timely manner.

Chapter 11: The Future of Data Science and Where It Will Go From Here

Before we end this guidebook, we need to take a look at an interesting topic that we come across when it comes to data science. And this idea is what we can do with data science in the future. There are already a lot of different tasks and models that we can use with the help of data science, but the future of this industry and the things that we will be able to do in the next few years, especially when we combine it together with artificial intelligence and machine learning, there are unlimited possibilities of what we are going to see. Let's take a look at some of the possible outcomes and uses of data science that we may see in the future.

Regulations for the industry

The first area that we need to explore when it comes to the future of data science is how it is going to come with regulations. With all of the data that the internet and other sources are generating all of the time, and the pace is likely to just accelerate all of the time, we need to focus a bit on the security of this informations. Companies need to be smart about the data they collect, and the amount of security that they put around this data. It is not going to do them much good if they collect this info, and then customers get angry because the data is not used in the proper manner.

In the next few years, it is pretty reasonable to expect that more and more regulations on how this data is collected and stored. For example, the European General Data Protection Regulation in 2018 was brought into play to protect individuals and their data from big companies and required any company that collected data on their customers to meet certain regulations on safety and security of that information.

The various activities of regulation are going to be important because they ensure that the company is not going to act in a bad manner and that they make sure to keep the best interests of the customers in mind. This helps them to keep the customers happy in the process while protecting the information that they want to use to improve their business. In all honesty, you will find that it is in the best interest of the company to work with safety and security in mind because it increases the amount of trust that your customers have in you.

Adding in more artificial intelligence

When it comes to data science, you can't go very long without hearing something about artificial intelligence, especially when it comes to machine learning and how this is going to combine together with the analysis that you do with the information. The way that machine learning works are going to get a system to learn how to do certain actions and behave on its own, without the programmer having to be present or without them having to write out every part of the code step by step.

Artificial intelligence is a big buzz word that comes with data science and many parts of business right now, and it is likely that this is something that is going to gain more power and steam as time goes on. As we are able to see some more benefits that go along with this over the next few years more companies will start to understand how artificial intelligence and data science are able to work together, and they will jump on board with it as well.

There are many ways that artificial intelligence is going to help out in the world of data science that we are working with. It can help with analyzing the data that we want to use to make smart business decisions. And it is also going to be used in many of the new products and services that are going to be offered in the future. This is a big place where data science and artificial intelligence are going to come together to make a world of difference. We are likely to see that data science points us to more artificial intelligence and more machine learning, and this is going to make a big change in our lives as well.

A virtual representation of real-world objects

Another thing that is likely to become more widespread over the next few years in the world of data science is going to be the idea of digital representations of physical objects that we see in real life, and these objects are going to be powered by the capabilities that come with artificial intelligence. These technologies are going to be used by businesses all over in order to help them solve real-life business problems no matter where that company is located throughout the world.

The pace of real-time innovations may have been something that seemed impossible in the past, but it is definitely something that we can focus on now, and you will find that these kinds of innovations are going to accelerate with some of the more advanced technologies that are likely to come out over the next few years as well.

Machine learning and neural networks are going to be used to help out with these applications, and new algorithms may be developed to help handle all of this. Both applications of virtual reality and augmented reality are already giving way to some big transformations in this kind of field. It is likely that there will be more breakthroughs in these areas, and in more, in the next year, and it is believed that the machine to human interaction is going to improve because of all these factors coming together. Of course, we will also see a rise in the experiences and expectations of humans when it comes to these digital machines and systems they are using.

The world of edge computing

It is also likely that the world of IoT is going to grow more and more into the future and as a result, something that is known as edge computing is going to just gain in popularity. With the hundreds of thousands of devices that we can work with, and even all of the sensors that are out there, we are collecting as much data as possible and then analyzing it to help businesses find that it is worth their time to work with data processing more and that it is much better to make sure the analysis of the data is going to happen as close to the data origin as possible.

The reason that this is so important is that it is going to really change up some of the methods used when it is time to consume the data, and can even change up the way that companies are going to collect their data, the type of data the company decides to consume, and we will see some huge changes in all of it within the coming years.

During this time, edge computing is going to start seeing a rise in popularity compared to what it does now. Edge computing is important because it is going to make it easier for a company to maintain a good amount of proximity to the source of their information. The closer that the business is able to get to the information source, the more accurate the information will become, the more information they will be able to get their hands on, and the more relevant the information is because they can gather the information right when it comes out, rather than somewhere down the line.

We will also find with the world of edge computing that some common problems, like bandwidth, connectivity, and latency. Edge computing and a bit of cloud technology are really seen quite a bit with data science and will provide us with a coordinated structure that will simulate a paradigm of the service-oriented model that we want to use.

In fact, one of the predictions that we have seen in IDC is already going to predict some of the following things. In fact, one statement about this is going to predict, "By 202, new cloud pricing models will help us to service-specific analytics workloads and will help contribute to 5X higher spending growth on a cloud vs. on-premises analytics." With this in mind, we can think about how much power this data science already has, and how much we are going to be able to use this in the future to help businesses beat out the competition and gain the best results in the process.

As you can see, there are already a lot of possibilities of what we are going to see when it comes to the world of data science and how it is likely to change in the future. This is an exciting field that has had its ideas around for some time, but the way that it is used, and the popularity of it, is growing like crazy. Being able to get in and learn about data science and how it works now before things go too crazy, can make a world of difference in the process as well, and will ensure that companies can be on board when things change to benefit them even more than before.

Conclusion

Thank You for making it through to the end of *Python Data Science*, let's hope it was informative and able to provide you with all of the tools you need to achieve your goals whatever they may be.

The next step is to get started by seeing how data science is going to be able to work for your business. You will find that there are a lot of different ways that you are able to use the large amount of info that you have access to, and all of the data that you have been able to collect over time. Collecting the data is just the first step to the process. We also need to make sure that we are able to gain all of the insights and predictions that come out of that informations, and this is where the process of data science is going to come into play.

This guidebook has taken some time to explore what data science is all about, and how it is able to help benefit your company in so many ways. We looked at some of the tasks that data science is able to help out with, what data science is and how to work with the life cycle of data, the future of data, and so much more. This helps us to see some of the parts that come to data analysis, and even how beneficial gathering and using all of that information can be to grow your business.

But this is not the only step that we can work with. We also need to take this a bit further and not just collect the data, but also be able to analyze that data and see what information it holds. This is definitely a part of the data science life cycle, but it deserves some special attention because, without it, the data would just sit there without being used.

In this guidebook, we worked with the Python coding language and how this was able to help us to work through all of that data, collecting models and more, so we could actually learn something useful and make predictions about the data as well. This guidebook spent some time introducing Python and how it works and then moved on to some of the best libraries that you can use to not only write codes in Python but to use

Python to work on the different models for analyzing the data you have.

Data science is a great thing to add to your business, and it can help you to make sure customer satisfaction is high, that waste is low, that you can make more money and can even help with predictions in the future, such as what products you should develop and put out on the market. But learning all of this is not something that just happens on its own. Working with data science, and adding in some Python language and the different libraries that are included with it can make the difference. When you are ready to work with Python data science to improve many different aspects of your own business and to beat out the competition, make sure to check out this guidebook to help you get started with it right away.

Description

Are you ready to gain a competitive edge over other companies in your industry jumping onto trends before anyone else even knew they were a possibility? Do you want to make sure that your product development ends up with something that is going to be an instant success on the market, rather than something that fails? Could your company stand to improve customer satisfaction, less time wasted, and more efficiency?

If any of these questions sound like something that you would like to see improved in your business, and you feel like this lack is harming your business, then it is time to take a look at what data science can do for you! With the help of collecting lots of information about the industry and economy around you, as well as about your customers, you can find powerful insights that will propel your business to the top.

This guidebook is going to provide you with all of the information that you need to learn more about data science, what this process is all about, and how you can use the Python language to put it all to work for you!

Even if you have no idea how to program or any idea of what to do with all of that data you have been collecting, this guidebook will give you all of the tools you need to be successful!

Some of the exciting topics that we are going to explore in this guidebook concerning Python data science includes:

- What is data science?
- Some of the basics of the coding language, including how to download the code and the basics of coding for the first time.
- Some of the best Python libraries to use with data science including Jupyter Anaconda, Pandas, and WinPython.
- The common tasks that we can complete with data science.
- The difference between structured and unstructured data and when to use each of these.
- What will happen with data science and where it will take us from here in the future.

Working with data science is becoming even more prevalent as the years go on, and businesses all over the world, and in many different industries, are using this to help them see more success. Whether you want to make predictions, provide better customer service, or learn other valuable insights about your business, data science with the help of Python, can make this happen. When you are ready to see what Python data science can do for your business, make sure to check out this guidebook to get started.